Caribbean Blues
& Love's Genealogy

poems

DANNABANG KUWABONG

© 2008 Dannabang Kuwabong

Except for purposes of review, no part of this
book may be reproduced in any form without
prior permission of the publisher.

We acknowledge the support of the Canada Council for the Arts for our publishing program and the Government of Ontario through the Ontario Arts Council.

 Canada Council   Conseil des Arts   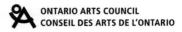 ONTARIO ARTS COUNCIL
for the Arts   du Canada   CONSEIL DES ARTS DE L'ONTARIO

Cover design by Heng Wee Tan

Library and Archives Canada Cataloguing in Publication

Kuwabong, Dannabang, 1955–
    Caribbean blues and love's genealogy : poems / Dannabang Kuwabong.

ISBN 978-1-894770-50-7

    I. Title.

PS8571.U89C37 2008   C811'.54   C2008-903384-1

Printed in Canada by Coach House Printing

TSAR Publications
P. O. Box 6996, Station A
Toronto, Ontario M5W 1X7
Canada

www.tsarbooks.com

Dedicated to:

Hawa Kuwabong
Delimwini Kuwabong
Angtuongmwini Kuwabong
Mwinidiayen Kuwabong
and the Ekɔla Clan

Contents

Book One: Caribbean Blues
Preamble: To My Caribbean Sisters   1
Child at Sea-Junctions   4
Arriving in Nanny's Country: Jamaica   6
Barbados
        Day I   15
        Day II   16
        Day III   18
        Day IV   19
Guyana
        Georgetown—Day I   22
        Georgetown—Day II   25
        Georgetown—Day III   26
        Georgetown—Day IV   29

Book Two: Love's Genealogy
Mapping   33
Love Throttles   35
Along the Spine   36
Before the Silent Gate   37
What the Eyes Say   38
Our Memorial   39
Behind Empty Silence   40
We Seek the Voice of Shadow   41
The Call   42
Commitment to Stone   43
Eating the Fruit   44
Face the Wall   46
Isolation at the Pool   47
At the Rodeo   48
How Beautiful   49
Remnants   50
Waiter at Passion's Table   51
Vigil at Death's Point   52
La Rumba   54
Rule of Fear   56

In the Mandala   58
Groping Ghosts   60
Among Forgotten Cynosure   61
No More Loon Calls   62
Catching the Passing Wind   63

Book Three: Miscellaneous Adventures
In Memory of a Fetus   67
Teaching English in UPR   69
Crushing Mangoes   70
My Last Testament   71

Book One

Caribbean Blues

Preamble:
To My Caribbean Sisters

I

I hear "wailing / wailing locked in the system" (Cynthia James)

to muzzle the mouth   is not to muzzle the sound
with cyanide of words   in your native calabash

                for the grating
                of broken teeth
                the tightened clench
                of bony wrists
                          still pumps blood
                              into dry presences

the turgid veins climb unto porous secrets of life and narrate many tomorrows and tell of passions yet unknown in the open gourd at rocky Blanchisseuse

II

                    the ocean foams
              the sea cleans everything
        along these rocks
where washerwomen create
forgetfulness
in broken palms

III

when cloudy midnight arrives   when storm covers night
the little star will yet outstay   keeping vigil at dawn
their pompous uncertain noon   there will be no cockcrow

the calabash lock will fall on the rock of okra and shatter to the
sound of life's hum where cobwebbed gourds echo amplified
meanings between the tap and sound of wooden keys.

there your feet will lead the dances of life at the feast of sorrow

IV

the single wail at noon   is not the "lonely pilgrimage with pain

                upon empty tarmacs
                   by the seaweeds
                      at midday

V

now you crawl across forgotten   gutters
into these plazas of discord
green gutter-weeds in your hair

        your language of mud rising
        pierce the ears of noisy gendarmes
        of the word made

                                  silent

        drunk with power of mind-walls
        keeping vigil over graveyard griots
        whose ghost abandon the flesh of words to them

VI

                    in our search for darkness
                    you are the fireballs forgotten
                    in our zeal to hide light

                    you become the feared fireball

the knife that cuts cord from womb
                            all else is pan and panic
                            all else is the loss of
                                                rage
ends in rags

VII

all else is "wailing / wailing locked in the system"
ahhh—waiting birth at dusk . . .

Child at Sea-Junctions

                                  I am that child of leftover falcon feed
I crawl from hidden bushes
crossing by leaf on raging tides

here I stand feet first
hands cup sanguine waves
back to my lips' innocence
and hiss of a pierced heart
                            S i n g i n g
songs:
let all who hear shout a—mina!
                      in the green brine that froths
                      penitent before unwilling gazes
                      my skull-cup of Crusoe's Friday
                      my necklace of Columbus's ribs
                      quilts these iodized seas
let all who hear groan a—mina!
                      I come seeking
                      names for faces
                      I come seeking
                      whispers from silences
                      I come seeking
                      meaning in madness
                      and hear only the sighs of the Sargasso
let all who hear hiss a—mina!
                      and chant with me:
                                  fleurs, fleurs, fleurs,
            fleurs
                          fleurs de sacrifice
            fleurs
                          fleurs de sanctité
            fleurs
                          fleurs yeux de la Mama Solitude

                          in the middle
                          of the battle
                          among the cutting cane

let all who chant hear a—mina!
                         for I am Solitude's foetus
                         wringing my birthblood
                         linking my birth waters
                         to the mouth of Rio Negro
let all the people say a—mina
let somebody say a—mina
                         my mouth is cold
                         my lips are sealed
                         and struggle is the womb of my words
let somebody say A—Men
                         my beginning here is not of flesh
                         my beginning here is not of bone
                         my beginning here is just a grunt
                         pain of loss in a wandering cloud
                         across these broad lakes——still
                         framed between falcon's claws
                         across these broad lakes——still
                                   and the people gather
                                   under the smiling ackee
                                   sipping tamarindo with pacha
                                   staring away
                                   stirring
                                   dreaming
let the people shout:
             im suun kom / but sun de kwenkyi
             im suun kom / but muun no shain
only pan heat crawls on watery skins
licking the torn flags on broken poles
only dream chants drip from broken lips
                                         the song is gone
across a boiling sea
             the memory rises from mountain tops to meet me

child of falcon feed
child of falcon feed
at the sea's junction

        let somebody shout A——Ba.

Arriving in Nanny's Country: Jamaica

I

arriving in Nanny's world
you must be pronunciation
coming to Cudjoe's world
you must be translation
not with the noise of words made into flesh
but in the shade of flesh made into words
so I begin in spirit tongue
bowing before the ackee root
listening to voices from my foremothers

Ja ma ka

Jaa maang kaa

Jaa maang Ng kaa

Jaa maang Ng ka

Jamaa kaa

                      Throw me here

                So it is me who watched

                 So it is me you watched

               So it me you emptied out

               People see, look, observe

beneath the ackee roots   where Sugbal Ngmeelee lies entombed
we boiled calallo   Nanny and Namuuma

they watched me, caught me, emptied me upon this rock above waters
it is a long story with lots of spaces without words
but all words have meaning
all carry the load of my pulse
all run to me beneath this limestone
of long mountain

I sit beneath the tamarind
I smell my rebirth at dawn
beneath these ashes of blue mountain
I smell burnt flesh among ruins
I see the kambonse of ashanti
dragging my forebears to Edina
I hear the kambonse of ashanti bargaining
the flesh of my forebears at Oguaa
with those that do not know my name

those that do not know ackee
those that do not know calallo
those that do not know tamarind
those that do not know sorrel
those that do not know waakye
those that creep from forest shadows
to steal me here

these are memorialized as my heroes
I call them by name: heroes of my misery hear this:
when you hear Jamaica
it is me you meaning
when you say Jamaangka
it is me you calling
when you shout Jamaankaa
it is me you gazing at

    I am the foundation bone
    of this land of misty blues
    I am the gnarled tap root
    in this limestone of wailing echoes
    where cut tongues thrust
    through the rasp of broken teeth

    somewhere in these maroon caves
    sunsets begin a nanny march
    buttocks rising across souls
    leaping on watery roofs

II

    the sun's stare
           blazes images from the savannah
                    floating
                         across long mountain valley

  puffing
                    above blue mountain river
                    the sound of panic recedes
                    in these dread of locks
                    there are no oval galleys
                    beneath these roars of surface
                    only slow gyration is vigil
                    keeping open memories of doors

III

so   in the months of mangoes and ackees
so   in the months of tamarind and callaloo

what a date
what a month
what a year

I descend the ladder
from the iron bird
pen webbed in my hair
notebook clutched in my hand
I am recognized
by an unction of days

IV

so I must begin my discourse of smiles
walaahi talaahi
what a day
what a year
what a homecoming

I ask you all sitting there
what is the tone of homecoming?
what is the mood of recognition?
what is the tone of smiling?
bone marrow and cartilage
vibrations of the occiput
looking, seeing, knowing
the curved rays to rebirth

there are no hidden pathways beneath the forest of my dreams. where there is dust. dust can copy the thrust of foot if wind stays still. footprints can be made. wind comes as a scream. scuttles on corrugated water chests. dead beneath the rust of fallen leaves. and these wails will never turn to screams again. screams. pull below utterance and glinting eyeballs on the rock. eternally cleansed by salty waves. what. what, can my yawn then catch in thickness of mist vapor of departures. vapors of beginning:

come unto me the voice beckons
you are detective
you are directive
show me meaning
show me crossing
beneath horizon of memory
begin:
un-name the unnamed
in these hollow sockets
rotating in a pounding skull
light the blazes
beneath the tunnels of night

                              sing the chorus
                    between the corridors of tales
                              ashes redeem all
                             water redeems all
                    from the cracks of broken circles
         and silence shall no longer reign in our terror
         and leaving will no longer march on empty songs

                    how then to re-vise my false steps
                          the word: con-cent-rate
                          again: con-cent-rate
                    rage cannot fix the age of gaze
              words cannot mend the break of links

                                    so. so. so
                             in my dazed pupil
                           all is mire and green
                    in these horizons of blue shadows

V

I look. I look. I look.
I forget my hunger for knowing

for beneath these bridges of shades
no flood waters rise again
here with wasps of fortune

not knowing what moves me
                              is knowing what stops me

            between motion and stillness
            movement halts before time
            stillness starts without time

time the whirlpool of memory
where red sunrays
betray neither dawn nor dusk
only redness of my weary eye

VI

I hear cockrow in the skies
I rise in the belly of the plane

it was not like that for Namuuma
it was not like that for Dabarema

it was not like that for them
who fell to the asante raids at dawn

you who ride the monsoon
you who harvest the harmattan
you who seek toe-prints
of those chained to the rock above water
only tongue-prints of memory remain
in the taste of aleefu in ackee

dropping from hibiscus
dropping at these paths
whirling forests and deserts
echoes the fearful cry
drowning the victor's song

sinks. sinks. sinks. sink in these damp bellies of rocking confusion.
waves. smells. sink
clang of ankle bones. flesh on hook to wood. float above snapping
fangs. sink.
everywhere. beneath bedrock. salt. sea-maids raise catafalques of
history. spirits sit waiting for breaking of seals —five now. and
shabine breaks only rum seals. water bites his skin across empty
steel drums.
                                                            sink.

circling dreams of lost roots
rising solitudes of newness

                                                                                                  sink.

agaist virgin wives

                                                                                                                             sink.

against virgin daughters

                                                                                                                             sink.

against virgin sisters
                    blood tides still flow
as un-offered sacrifices above board
                          only these un-dead red threads
                floating in snow storms
                        shall be witness to my beginnings

and there shall be no end to my vigils of wailing. laughter.

wail. where water coffins have run aground on these rocks of Montego Bay. souls. lurking on moaning ground seeking heartease. souls. lurking between thin white sheets on dusty shelves. waiting for foreday morning.

look around. look around. pen cannot write every site. word cannot tape every sound trapped in the belly and spine. strapped to shifting sands of a return to the genesis of these four corners of the seas of history.

                                                                                                                             sink.

            I rise. I rise and say!
            come opiel
            give me the drink of clouds
            tell me:
            what does your curios eye
            bulging through your bone see?

VII

I am blinded by the noisy pages of history
I am infracted through the silence of definitions
but I know somewhere
through these misty rays
a skeleton clutches spirit
a body seeks marrow
where the skulls lie cold
under the baobabs of flame-balls

VIII

smell of shadows
burning flesh, burning flesh
bones beneath the seabed
rise to this dance of dreams
hold my hand over surf

for though I have not found it
these par-roast herbs
essence above smoke
tamarind pods open to flesh tunnels
ackee is history of welcome

at my gate of memory
terror fears the failure of words
and what comes after the hurricane roar of commands without
authority
only blank silence of the stare prevails
in the cell of the womb of memory:

I climb over
and walk carefully
over a weakening bridge
in the silent shadow of Nanny
as she gazes in bewilderment

                                        over these distant peoples
                                         who tramp day and night
                                         to claim other Englishes
                                       to Little England then I went
to Barbados then I came
seeking assurances
from Nelson's ghost
beneath a shrine at Trafalgar Square
where the smell of khebab
blends with the aromas of a lagoon
floating against the harmattan
floating towards the Gulf of Guinea

Barbados

Day I

here
there
everywhere
no (w)here (t)here

so it was this noon—after: singing songs of pepper eaters
a little red-robin
floats upside down
watching a dying daisy
in a rabbit's teeth
singing of rocks at sea edges:

Albion found the sun on these rocks
Celts kindled their twilight here
the Africans were chained here
on these spirit rocks of Arawaks
jutting into this blue-green sea

what can a little birdie eye see
except dead worm on the road?
what worms can breed in the rock?
where there is no humus?

sea water sterilizers all.
sea water preserves it all
so these knee jerks at all
into a violent sea of words
how do we pronounce a name
for a rock of emptiness
suddenly peopled by children of the sun
suddenly peopled by children of the snow

swisssh! swissh! leather
carries scraps of skin on its tips
and quivering Dagaaba look at the rock
look at rising dust on their lips
listen to the roar of their words
hiss into the silence of rocks of silence

Day II

all paths scramble
to Trafalgar Square
you cannot lose direction
around these masquerades
prostrating at crossroads
chanting:

come
oh come all ye faithful
tired and also bored
come to Little Albion
from every sudden corner
come

accept from rough westward
where to gaze is to be seen
to see faces unrecognized
to hear voices unrehearsed
to cross out lakes of labels
to reach the cave of rock offering

come
un-mask your free spirit
when the face disappears
where flesh becomes spirit
come
where foot no longer cares
pleasure begins
in the footfalls
where water separates
origins from originals
and sea brine bleaches all to grey
here, sea water lashes history away
here the *toubabs* of terror
have nailed the *toubabs* of death
to this shade beneath a rock

we have erected a shrine
to sunshine and tan
come, join in the offering
the people dance
the people jive and grind
in this shindig of pain
what more could your dollar buy
on the morning of her naming?

Day III

they mumbled before the shrine
to Nelson their god
before the temple square at Trafalgar
many had forgotten Yocahu
and the conch call of Antah Setsarakoo
and the lamentation of Chatoyer

red flames announce the prophetess
she slouches out from Cave Hill
from the tamarind grove
her voice rises with the blue zemis:

Baa ba do! Baa ba do! Baa ba do!
and the supplicants rise in unison
Baa ba do! Baa ba do! Baa ba do!
(re)-member-ing the call of Opiel

relief sizzling from parched lips
creating a new sound: Baa ba dos
as they circled the rock for two days
naming the silence and the stone

Day IV

in the morning
mangoes fell
in the afternoon
mangoes fell
in the evening
flying fish flew
into the empty pans
sitting on empty hearths

how to respond
how to respond
me then to the promontory
legs across the sea
hands across the ocean
looking for sequences
in maturity of ginep
in tamarind's sour-sweetness
in names on museum boards

a voice comes across the Sargasso
I say wait not waste nor waist
you who seek solitude upon a rock

a voice echoes from the Caribbean
I say If not sip or flip you chance
upon a mouth seeking silence

a voice sobbing from the Atlantic
seeking silence in a ward of words
refuses to call to me but wails:

they have chained you
to a desire to resist

they have chained you
to a desire to forget

they have chained you
to a desire to denounce

let sleeping dogs die
a cruel death of marrow dream

let sleeping gods die
a cruel death of worship dreams

for crop-over time don com
and master day don do

let planter forget
the neat slice of thin flesh
between elbow and armpit

on the noon of cutting cane
and accept bottled genii
where Barbados must rise

in the aftermath of *Jonconu*
in the monsoon of carnival
I grind my path to moaning ground

where Shango in Krishna pose
awaits my homecoming
in a feast of rosary beads
and turbans in a basin of water

in the "palace of peacocks"
by *the four banks
of the river of space*
I must search for the "eternal genesis"
between the mad
and the maddening

in the month of hurricanes
Columbus's ghost guides me

through the narrow nipples
of the three breasts of earth
to the Orinoko of Walter Raleigh
where the Damerera dies to sweeten my coffee

between the sweetness of treacle
and the flow of slashed wrists
in the pain of cane
all smiles report the pang of gold
On the boat to sweet Demerara
Where water defines the span of life

singing:

"Lick an lock up don wid
Hurrah fuh Jin Jin
Lick and lock up don wid
Hurrah fuh Jin-Jin"
(Ian McDonald)

Guyana

Georgetown—Day I

brown water in your canals
where edoes love to sip
stay with me
drum my song
in the gargle
of your flow

the pavements of Robestone are wide
the sidewalks of Quamina street green
mystery stalks
these brown deepness
it shifts behind bushy brows
into an emptiness of lost dreams

everywhere the people say:
here water defines the angles of abodes

every resolute acceleration
breaks sudden before horse-carts
breaks sudden before drinking cows

everything the people do:
water defines the angles of abodes

come, let me show you Georgetown
you mean, Georgetown not Jonestown?
Georgetown misses an abdicating king
as sullen Victoria frowns away
before this gurgling brown sea
her silence is assured rule
with a broken upper lip
her hands helpless beside her
weighed down by blood homage

so here she stands, still frowning
to be restored before a leaking court

everywhere the people chant:
water defies the flow of cases at night

everywhere the people sigh:
water defines the concourse of life

this here is Republic Street
where masquerades stop
for release from public masks
here, we walk sideways
facing the silence at Starbroek
imploding in sweet Demerara rum
cracking coconuts without milk

everywhere the people say:
water defines the discourse of truth

you asking where then is El Dorado?
Yes, this is Raleigh's dream relayed
yes, Behn's lost Eden with golden leaves
yes, the El Dorado by Orinoko

everywhere the people dream:
water defines the color of distant dreams

my awakening! my awakening!
such dreams had named me
when they met Cara Mansa
at savannah Edina
the dream of Costa d'Elmina
with stone and mortar
they built castles of power
and sought the gold in salt waters

thank you sister

I polish my shoe
in fresh donkey-dung
I gaze upon the golden smiles

behind faces that stretch unseeing
pushing along Starbroek market
remembering Nanville market
knowing now why Victoria frowns

for everywhere the people say:
water defines the fall of queens.

THE HAMILTON SPECTATOR

44 Frid St. | Hamilton, ON | L8N 3G3 | thespec.com

Ted Brellisford
Photographer

- **t.** 905.526.3338
- **f.** 905.526.1395
- **c.** 905.971.3207
- **e.** tbrellisford@thespec.com

Georgetown—Day II

stranger looking for your home
you must rise early
and wash your face
with the white vapors of our dawn

tread gently on the mist
grey, it smothers all green
gray, it blunders all brown
grey, it shelters foetal gnats
float along Demerara channels

stranger I say
you must beat the rising sun
in a blanket of birdsong
while eyes silently speak
behind this wide silence
of quivering lips
as you gaze without seeing beyond
oily water beneath flooded bridges

so here I stand in birdsong
somewhere along Lucytown
with a drowned doll's leg
defying watery pulls
the yawning gutter-man
sees nothing but rain

Georgetown—Day III

birds go to sleep
donkeys lick their wounds

curry carries the evening
on its yellow shoulders

limers lime lamp-posts
I step through light into night

there are no masquerades here
there are no monuments here

only forgotten ghosts call
and all that moves rises

limers lease spaces below shop lamps
eyes roaming everywhere

where the sweet sweat of the old
freeze in the breeze of fear

cast by perfumes of youthful muscle
and the threats of thumpers
in their troopers and tanks

beyond these edoe banks

    and water glistens under grass shadows

        here is Regent Street
           stretched through Lacytown
               where Red Thread does Kyk-over-all
               and flies flap fast and fall
                  before these dark crevices
                     of moss guarded walls

grease trickles along footpaths
no-one notices the spurts of life
except surprised tadpoles
preparing to shed some tails
night crawls like wounded snake
no, like an abandoned cloud
over the horizon beyond Demerara
Georgetown scuttles away
leaving night's begotten few
clotting around broken bridgeheads
moving away from Brickdam

only Wellington street remains poised
watching
watching
waiting
for the young
for the bold
for the beaux
for the restless
or by *General Hospital*
poised astride broken stone walls
whispering

water courses beneath the broken walls

somewhere in the sudden curb
life begins to murmur
Strand Cinema unpacks a role
calls to us by name and act
calls our innocence into its space
to *Indecent Proposal II*
where *Indecent Proposal I* failed to persuade

water rises and falls in South Street Canal
it cannot touch the pleasure boat without sail

                    I have no theory of pleasure
                    pleasure is in the watching
                    pleasure is in the walking
                  to Camp Street then I trek
              here, laws protect the unwanted
        in nightmares behind walls
            all around the corrugated steel
                juke boxes preach sweetness
                    but water like their tears
                        stand shimmering before Leslie Jacobs
                            who dresses people with Europe
                        when sun seeks payment everywhere

brown water is the root of these mahoganies
brown water is the green of these "mankany"

the pavements of Brickdam are beachy
all in the midst of silence
except the coqui song
                keeping vigil with Rodney's ghost
                        heaving above cross
                                hovering above Hadfield Cathedral
            and sits in the unnamed chapel
                    beside a stone of Kyerie Eleison
                        beside his marble Materna Dei
                                interceding for a nation
                                    at the brink of a whirlpool

            kyerie eleison, kriste eleison, kyerie eleison
            through the gold paved teeth of Guyana

                        I turn and head for the silence of my cell
            and behind me
I hear a loud burp saying:

the   smiles   of   Guyana   are   paved   with   gold   . . .

Georgetown—Day IV

                                  Red Thread has moved again

again innocence threatens
our wake-up dream desires

all   that   is   left   are   broken   boxes
struggling/for/space

                  beneath an open sky

the trio's motto reads clear
written in the channels of sweat
flooding tomorrow's smiles:

"never write die until the bones are dust"

Red Thread is no Red Threat as they say
            Red Thread is end of innocence
                      Red Thread is beginning of life

here in Hadfield Street
        they kneel gathering red drops from sand
            when the parcel opened up Rodney
                close to this brown water
                    they blend their blood lines
                        with those who refused to die of cane

but chose life in death by sea

        I sit in Brickdam Catholic Life Centre
thinking if Red Thread were not
what would become of our blankness

                              stranded by silent canals of words
would there be other town-criers
to join Ian in Kyk-Over-Al
or only urban-prowlers
  kicking over all?
                  in my confusion

in my confusion
I turn my face to a rock
and fax my dreams
to a masquerade of naming
where to stand tall
is to be little of somewhere
the shadow takes away the coolness
leaves only the smell of heat
where salt water
does not whiten the skin
in downtown Hamilton

I stroll a defeated lord around Jackson Square at midnight before dawn

I ride on the nipples of thunder
I answer her summons of wonder
son of saltwater moles
I open my heart tributaries
to touch her stowed pain

I yearn
I yearn
for a rocking of peace
under the weight of sundown
to echo drums of sunrise

through these nodes around the nipples
I sip before dusk
bitter juices before milk
draw out my destiny
from this stone of pain

I yearn
I yearn
for a rocking of love
under the sundown of shadows
echoes of drums at sunrise
or wailing the end of love's genealogy?

Book Two

Love's Genealogy

Mapping

I walk
between Queen and Queesndale
and brood on how
King competes with Main
to see which reaches Gage Park first

but before I turn on Victoria south
I hear silent footfalls
I measure my shadow steps
between their pillars of distances
I fear I cannot retrace my own steps
in the whirlpool of stares
beneath a hanging tree

thus fearful
I turn quickly on Emerald south
head for the East Mountain brow
crushing eternity beneath Adidas soles
taking the steps as they appear
I hear the chant in the forest around me

"Pink is the inner circle
it must empty into whiteness
where unwanted copper
drown in fake falls
beneath the office of passports
in honest Square of Jackson"

I knock too late on memory's door
summon dreams long dead gone
to witness my chilled emotions
the witness turns her back
creep into memory's cave
through narrow pathways
of the dungeons of age
I run, fingering a faded dream

under a crippled maple tree
I squat on a root and eat pine cones
I chant songs of desire
curios kids
homeless elders
adventurous youths
surveillance cops
circle hesitatingly
asking without speaking
what was all this about?

Love Throttles

"Love does not throttle you"
You are so sure of your statement
You argue:

you arouse it standing
slowly you let your throat be grabbed
then you gasp and fall slowly, slowly
and sink in the weight of its sighs

I am your cartographer
mapping your terra nova
seeking to grasp in my clasp
the sound of moaning torsos
the instant of muscular joys
the glints of serenity
of the eye of dreams

then you are cauterized
dipped in the color of dreams
dozing on notions of a return
my voyage to the tundra
disentangles the mesh of doubts
that ties these limbs of colors

neither then holy nor mad
in your mouth of mumbled repeats
my name becomes evacuated despair
without language or sound
I read it in the sterile smile of parting
your eyes reflect your voice
drawing me, amazed into your depths
I crawl over the threshold
below the hanging bower

a shivering along the spine

Along the Spine

here then I squat like a frog
with no shiver in my spine
drawing emptiness
beneath a ceiba without shade

blackbird seeking night shades
I flutter in your shadow of silence
caught in your web of words
seeking shelter for my words
but others' wisdom reel and seal the exits
leaving only steamy entrances
where cicadas gather as offering

here then I squat frog-like
drawing images, chanting:
float image float
be a mirage behind my emotions
like a string of cowries
decorate my antlers
for I will not sprinkle ashes
around this corpse
nor chant desire to
to this cold sole

to this cold sole stranded
somewhere
in the wombs of laughter
seeking the larynx to life
watching you watching
what the sons of night
do to the daughters of light

I am the gatekeeper to our molding gateways of desire

Before the Silent Gate

come, I will sit with you
dream daughter of the moon
I will let your drips of blood
soften these bones of resistance
call me to your deepness
lead me to journeys of my beginnings

for slowly the sun recedes into its rest
for slowly the city lights blink and blare
and one by one avenues distribute our doubts

so what if we gaze halfway to pinnacle hill
and only a faded sheet floats into our vision
on it may read:
"you dark zygote / in embryo gel / stapled to two sides
of retracting placentas / knock within / knock within
but there is no sound without / only the groan of puking"

what does it mean? I will ask you
what does it mean? You will ask me

we will sit above the bridge, legs entwined
playing sand games with our toes
waiting for the drizzle promised

gently your gaze will reveal a wind
forgotten by children of fire
I will retrieve meaning in your eyes

What the Eyes Say

broken and bent
beyond youth's turbulence
my spent spine grunts
beneath the yoke of feeling
dreams and memories of dreams
guide and guard each slow step
into formless nights
paralyzed on an empty bed

like a dry lemon peel in the wind
I stiffen and rot, hurricane of desire
beneath the long rain/reign of neglect
my form becomes formless
who will/can/should feel me now
hush is their wander/wonder word
as I prepare to possess
the red courtyard of their heaving

I shrivel, I shrivel, on these two (st)humps
return to infant beginnings
and all becomes twisted forgetfulness
only the proverb of me may remain
but nothing else shall be a memorial

except this crowding in the loin
except this pounding in the groin

Our Memorial

slowly we veer toward the edge
where there will be none to witness
edges that shift like chameleons
beneath a hurricane above water

words come hurtling, screaming
hollow blobs of flotsam
desiring fear, desiring voice
but silence is the noise in the ear
breaking, imploding to our star of loneliness

is the dawn of our trumpet come?
there are no new moons
there are no left-over twinkles
only the crowding in the head

finally we awaken to spirit call
at last water, fire, larva, and ice
have fulfilled the dream foretold
calling back is futile
for your sound or mine
remains locked within evaporated ideas

so we move our disgruntled feet at the edge
defenseless against these desires

Behind Empty Silence

you and I then have known
we must defend against desire
with these clipped wings we fly
through the thickening sounds
where words riot in labor to conceive

through this oily stagnancy
you at the edge of nothing
I at the start of nothing
mere distractions of refractions
through a total plunge
we may perhaps emerge into it
into our center of fertility games
sorting the sounds of moaning
streaming the screams of dying
clawing undergrowths of separate ways
toward the salt of passion on the brow

muted mutations of love
we may yet steal time present
stalk our future with wrinkles of our past
and sink in the silt of hold-backs
no tears to leave for our muted love

We Seek the Voice of Shadow

a wandering face
on a rainy day
is no serious joy
so we carry our tired feet
seeking the voice of shadow
beneath the lightning of others:

"dark clouds is not nightfall
the voice behind the face
determines the path
the gully beneath the belly
determines the cull-de-sac"

you my dear
the single wail in noon darkness
guides the lonely pilgrim
through the language of mud.

somatic prints of our dreams
where evenings come and stay
instructing our fingers
on the language of flesh:

"sail through the cracks of desire
drown in its stormy vortex
swirl, twist, leap beyond the earth
somewhere real rocks will fall
giving light pathways to your cave

pay heed: do not block the body's horizons
for your way forward is but a memory
thundering on a rainless day."

The Call

evenings have come and left
windy prints on these crowded beaches
noisy with silent promises

but under this frangipani
I remain in your shadow
a cicada luminous
awaiting the mating call

the half-moons rise and are called
in the descent of full moons
many names are lisped
to walk between the dusk and dawn
I am not among the fortunate

beneath the flaming tree
I peek through gathering clouds
as larks dance farewell to a sinking sun
and the coqui respond to the zest of night

I your noon-shade
await your call, hoping
hoping when you call to me
I will not hear the goodbye
but I will hear the dream-on

Commitment to Stone

Like a burnished moon, quartered
dodging between racing cumulus
unable to perform my task
I hide and wait for a peephole in your shadow
but a squinting minaret of an abbey
betrays my once existence

I who allows you free access to me
passionate larva proceeds after desire
floods every hidden alley
come, count the cracks on my skin

I wonder how still a chiseled stone
remains in me un-molten
as clods of memory swirl and recoil
recall every single heavy thud
of your bludgeon
behind your granite-clad face
afraid of a commitment to my stone

Eating the Fruit

behind your granite-clad face
afraid of a commitment to my stone
you look with fright at my toenails
and turn away changing colors
thinking how tonight
your purity will be impaled

it is five after midnight
even the frogs have sang goodnight
and here we sit on the edge
the bed a sepulcher of delayed delight
grows dim by shadows of your hair
flinging puzzled invitations

you rise up and go to the basket of fruits
retrieve a large banana and two granny apples
then you hand me a split avocado
the seed stares uncertainly at me
you stick the banana in your mouth
nibble slowly and smile
you leave the banana stranded between your teeth

then you breathe steam on the grannies
rub them against your thighs
then silently you give them to me
you return the avocado to the basket
surely, something must be wrong, I think
but you gulp the banana suddenly

you rise up and stand, yawning
a spidery removal of the clothes
reveals your environmental concerns
for between your smooth pylons
lies a glistering impenetrable jungle
overhanging swollen banks
of a slushy fly-trap and river

through which I must navigate
blindfolded and rushed

uncertain of the courage
with which I come to you
what if my paddle should break and I drown?
What if the trap leads to a bottomless well?
What if I fall in slow, dark, and never reach a stop?
you see my fear and smile while pointing
I shrivel in panic
I become a gasping slug
drooling, propped by two wrinkled tomatoes
I scurry to the bathroom and sob
You say softly: Men! you turn to hug a bear

Face the Wall

You speak softly:
comfort is the child of pain
long forgotten memories
kill their owner in their uprising
so I yield to what I give up

many moons have risen and died
when these same arms that calmed your quivers
now like pincers give you the shivers
scattering the rehearsed emotions
proffered in these stringy biceps
I coo and woo your welcome clasp
but arms that culled my exits
now like pincers bar my entrances

what can I say?
stranded in your face with a quizzical grin
I see my moves now as bald, lame and limpid
Lost in smiles of denials

Outside the flaming tree is ecstatic
Flings a petal on my bald spot
As the storm purifies its breathing
I look for you
You are not there
I am homeless in your shadow

Suddenly,
the panting phantoms of my dreams
reel and slide beneath my emptiness
they leave my puffed-up breast
hollow, a periwinkle between lips

I turn to face the wall
hands between my thighs

Isolation at the Pool

water falls from the rock above
beneath a pool clear and cold
gathers and swirls a welcome

slowly we step into its womb
you hold my hesitant hand
beckon, encourage, cajole
draw me to your chest in water
my nose trembles between your breasts
we float, we float, we splash about
careless of the rushing currents
our laughter echo through the crags
as goose pimples like many nipples
yield to the touch of icy fingers
I close my eyes and see visions

we leave the pool below, you first
and I, I forget my sprained knee
and like a bee at the scent of nectar
I buzz behind your skimps
we climb slippery slopes
hoisting ourselves by dangling roots
sweaty, we reach the second pinnacle

here isolation engulfs us
you spread-eagle on your back
I crawl on my knees toward you, smiling
you hand me a tube of cream
I squirt it on your body
gently I stroke and coax the swellings to go
jealous at the insects
that freely dive into you
and I your choice for the day
can only gaze in a daze and rage
into the depths I will never enter
because . . .
Suddenly it is time to go.
To make my vespers

At the Rodeo

Suddenly it is time
To make my vespers
I bow before your shrine
Burning sweet smoke
Peering with watery eyes
Listening for dream signals

Yet no voice rustles
An answer to my search
Why do I then yearn
to donate my very being at your altar?

At the rodeo of fertility games
You always are the tamer
Of these wild and turgid thighs
You mount one and come at full speed
And I lie paralyzed
Whimpering at the gates of action

After your collapse
I strain for a taste of the excitement
But you quickly dismount and flee
Laughing, laughing or sobbing

I roll over and out of the bed
I limp to the bathroom

How Beautiful

I roll over and out of the bed
I limp to the bathroom to think:
How beautiful the distance
Between desire and fulfillment

The oasis in the dessert
Is a mere mirage of trickling water
There is little comfort then
In a mouthful of sand
Where blood thickens into flesh
In this park of aborted loves
Then you see the invisible tree
It stands defiant in the dessert
Aloof
calling shadows of its branches
Grasping at moving shades
Beneath a disappearing sun

The invisible tree
It stretches out its roots
Breaking crust, breaking sand
Seeking an oasis where there is none

Tree at a distance: you say
Tree without leaves: you observe
Dance at sunrise
Dance at sunset
Dance at the howl of the winds
I see you bend
At the cave's mouth
Where I dangle my feet and wonder:

How beautiful the distance
Between you and the oasis.
Any other is a remnant

Remnants

how beautiful the night
that lies between you and me
as I strew dry peels of our dreams
upon the catafalque of comfort
whispering echoes of silence
circling shadows of memory

I chant les chansons de morte de l'armour

it is all souls day
but no smiling wraith
rises to meet me
at the doorstep to my dreams
only these cushion dents
body prints where you lay
hugging these feathery pillows
away from hairy warm arms

tentative, only the fading whiff
of your odor hangs tremulous
among forgotten garments
echoing your parsing
echoing the night
waiting to summon
waiter at passion's banquet
on the day desire is served on a platter

Waiter at Passion's Table

on the day desire lies on a platter
I will be the waiter
carrying canned desires
in green avocados
waiting behind the whispering door

the blade of love abandoned
will slash through these veins
the jinns of passion
will be the grinding stones
where promises of midnight
are ground into broken dreams

I will hear them say:
"at the center
he is granite
below
a silk cotton tree
memory recedes
hunters love eros
stretch out weary cudgels
soon depart
soon depart
soon forget
the cold peace he gave
the surety he promised"

and soon return
and soon return

stony dust cracks of their feet
wilderness in whites of the eyes
humming the songs of stone

prostrate
beneath mists of dreams
in a summer grave of passion.

Vigil at Death's Point

beneath these elemental surfaces
scarring our lines of hopes
spiritual births occur
binding our wounded dreams
to those that lack faith

our locations are not obligations
to stand vigil at death's point
moving away from love's futures
in this pentagon called Canada
chance is measured on the anvil of class

thus, the horn of excitement
that beckoned to me from afar
lies shattered under the anvil of pigment
and shred fulfilment basket of dreams

was the glitter of hopeful encounters
a mere meteorite of truth
on a stormy night of nightmares
is this conjuration of dawn
a harbinger of death in our binding act

we wretch between protestations
fall in the bitterness from our insides
while the world sniff snuff
to keep at bay the forces of fear

were we tripped then
in the day of laughter
our bowls of mirth shattering
on these pavements of pain
their contents emptied
blending in camwood juice
now sipped daily to nourish our bitterness?

Go in peace
daughter of heroines
this stony clay on our faces
will not reveal the mystery of the death
in which our love grew apart
we have looked for gates in goat entrails
but every twist closes a gateway
and the hand-bells shaken in the rain
the chants of the forefingers
no longer evoke images of peace
behind the mirrors of yesterday's dream
playing abandoned fertility games

I dream of the freedom
at the L'allegro in La Rumba
my feet strayed to the den

La Rumba

This night I say to myself:
"I will rise and lift my feet
To where bodies become disjointed
I will creep to Stilletto's
There to meet Loneliness
And teach my feet to Rumba
I will wear my mask of misery
And grind my waist to sounds of the Edge
I will lend my heart to Mambo
By deserted Tonic Lounge on King Street
Where cubanos are puffed on domingos

I will stand in a smoky corner
And peek at quivering bellies
Blurring my promises and oaths
To lose my practised s-ways
I will mop my brow and move on
I will grub at La Costa Nuova
Or take out at Shenai

This night I say to myself
I will rise up and run
To where bodies are jointed
I will enter Dizzy Weasel
Or weave among others at Funky Munkey
To look around preaching my needs
Through a tongue no-one hears
Warble my distress no-one hears
Wink my deliriums no-one sees
Tears of my dejections, no-one wipes

I will hallucinate in the heat
Of these unexplored desires
And no-one will recognize me
As I glitter in my darkness
To the dungeon paths of joy

I will wake up
In this cave without dreams
Where a cold embrace awaits
To cool this heated heart
Where love injects rejection
To where I have arrived

At these crossroads of desires
Where dreaded passion sits
Wielding the club of fear
Reading the signpost of confusion
To whispering crowds of loners
In this mansion of miserable un-fulfilment
In this mansion of unfinished desires
In this mansion of unfinished fulfilment
When the night ends
I will grope for a light that does not shine
Where the hammer strokes of fear rule the strong

Rule of Fear

through these fertility games of summer nights
in the jazzy streets of Hess Village
voices burst asunder
into nightmares of my hopes
cracks my parched brain and
flowers into seed
unconditional
blooming

the girl and the boy spread love on concrete
where there is no rain
unconditional
knowing

under these conditions
petals soon wither
a call, a whisper
soon a whimpering
in the silent spaces
of these cross-rhythms and saxophone
AAh!
To hide memories of the heart
from faces of the mind

here we sit
against a cold wall
wailing softly
into a blue sheet
as panic riots in cell membranes
seeking an alter-altar of fear
against death through passionate love
against death through careless love
against the ruins of a generation

"Oh!
The pain of fright, the fright of disgrace

                    the pain of result, the result of a seed
                                      invisible gnawing
                                in the cauldron of creation"

                              "in this transubstantiation
                             anything gullible can happen
                                          and wreck forever
                                  our carefully nurtured plot
                    to harvest flowers from our side-year"

                              "We could not surrender our minds
                             only the rhythmic throbs of our ribs
                              we could not surrender our bodies
                       only the rhythmic moves of our shadows"

                              "Through the hurricanes of promises
                                      liming against the steppes
                                      water clothing our desires
                                     limpid as the falling Niagara
                              crackling leaves of a dying forest
                               waiting for the return of thunder"

                                                "It never could be
                                              it was not meant to be
                                            to walk this tight-rope
                                            with okra-coated feet
                                                a dangerous dream

                                       we obeyed the rule of fear"

the memory recedes to Aibonito
in concrete paved Puerto Rico
to the night dance of frustrated feet
in a stony Mandala

                                    chanting hosannas to a waning
                                                                moon

In the Mandala

out of the Mandala then
I step between waving pines
I see glowing faces
mere or real shadows
behind fluttering flames
I listen for tunes of knowing
the praise song to La Luna Madre
somewhere to the south

she rises
dispels all cumulus
and the silent drum moans
between coqui calls
to daughters of Atabey
to the sons of Yúcahu
trembling before Ciguayo caves
awaiting words of wisdom
from grey-haired Maiakan

across Caribbean sea
halfway on these mountain slopes
I erect a checkpoint
between my mind's freedom
and the swiftness of the lips

what vision of the heart I carry
lurks like a frightened frog
in wrinkled ideas of history
silence as sentry
listening in silence to noise
of unuttered syllables
lodged in the memory of pain

to the northeast before sunset
the boulders as witnesses loom
awaiting the rise of night

I descend into pulse breaks
I sit, I wonder

on sound before the word
on echo before the sound
where my unuttered silence
scratches a bleeding heart

here in the center of the Mandala
love has no direction for desire
except the eternal turnings
that spread out before the dazed feet

I the silent visitor
seek noisy ground-holds
between soft hums of the heart
and memories of lamentations
I hear only the grate of granite
and thunder beyond the clouds

all around, all around
in the dark humid dusk
the voices recede, recede
into distances below valleys
trailing behind flute songs
of anomies of desires

I am stranded in the corners of night
assumes little
desires little
getting nothing
I slip and fall
I slip and fall
before three shadows at dawn
asking my *duma*
how come I keep straying
where others return
to their moments of joy
to their moments of silence?

I must arise and go forth
to the La Rumba
and soak my misery in spirit bottles

Groping Ghosts

I will grope for a light that does not shine
In this night as I strew
The dry petals of our dreams
Upon the catafalque of comfort
Whispering echoes of silence
Circling shadows of memories

Chanting mes chansons de l'amour
On this day of all souls
Without any smiling wraiths
That will rise and dance with me
Only these mattress dents
Will proclaim where her body rested
Hugging these stuffed bunnies
Away from my tentative tentacles

Thus after all
Only the fading whiff
Of her departing
Hangs a cloudlet of desire
In this coin of passion rack
Among forgotten cynosures

Among Forgotten Cynosure

Among forgotten cynosures
When that day starts
I shall be the waiter
Carrying a tamed gudgeon
In these green granny's
Waiting behind
A whispering door-nob

The knife of tense desire
Slashes through these turgid veins
Of soft deferment
Becomes the stone sacrifice
Where the promises of midnight
Are crushed into magma
Beneath mists of dreams.

No More Loon Calls

and so we obey the rule of fear!"
every starry night
every cloudy night
every sunny day
every cloudy day

I sit alone
By the same window
I pick alone
The same warm plate
I meant to share with you

I look alone
At the empty seat
I look again
At the set plate
There is no face
At the center of the space
There is no voice
To silence the quiet

"it seems so long ago
when through the cries of loons
you came at dawn or dusk
slipping through the sentries
of a garrisoned heart
silent like the message of a nipple
weaving webs of assurance
and I sprawled in the sand of your dream

your goodbyes corrupted me
showed me goodness
goodness without desire
but oh! That was so long ago
I sleep-walk around the house
Yearning to be wakened
By the soft fall of your heel
Listening for a whispered memory
Only crickets reward my desperations

Catching the Passing Wind

Only crickets rewarded my desperations
In the sweep of winds across the prairies
Over the tassels of wheat fields that stretch
To feed teeming millions in steaming ovens
I hurry across my failures

If only I could be yours
I will be your terra nova
For your invisible brush strokes
But I have made statements
Made plans for you to follow

though I yearn to be him
I must walk in the storm
I must thread the passing wind
Through this needle of collected hopes
Across the ice-storm terrain of desires
While this garden still is warm and moist
And sleeping men still dream

When the seeds take root
When the flowers bloom
When the petals open
And receive pollination
Let my love be the last dew drop
Flickering, hanging, tremulous
Before a crash under green shadows
Seeping through the soil
Of nourished astonishment"

Book Three
Miscellaneous Adventures

In Memory of a Fetus

pink paper played no part
yellow sheets stayed unruffled
white roles lay silent
inside the dusty air
within orange walls and doors
many faces sweat
hymen blood and water

"I knew you would come someday
I meant to prepare for that coming
but not this surprise touch and go
where strange faces wonder
I knew you would come someday
but not here behind blue doors
here glazed with others' urea

yes, there have been signs
yes, there were symbols
I hoped you would stay
and give me a chance
I believed you could stay
for me to nurture your love
now that is gone
with the messy secret
your sojourn in my heartbeat

how will I explain to Him
who spring in the rain
dreaming of that white mantel
a crude cuddle of supple limbs
a title to sit among others
will he understand?
but what about me?

the emptiness of your absence
gushing in red waters
from this marrow and hair
has no lamentation
so how can he feel what I feel

oh my departed unborn
oh my depleted womb space
you too did not desire
to be a number on the web
to be number on the vote

perhaps you saw right and said:
Ah! this hockey field
has no fairness
but I would have loved you
but I would have kissed you
called you by your name
but I would have held you
but I would have kept you
called you by your name
but you decided to peep and go

I am not bitter
I only sorrow in my womb
that as spirit now
I cannot hold you
in these arms
in these supple arms crossed
so ready to receive your embrace

my unborn one
so many things I would say to you
cannot now be thought of
only remember this as you go
I still carry you in my heart
the smell of colors
will always be there for you
the smell of live
will always bring back today and you
will always bring back today and you
and I will . . .

Teaching English in UPR

teaching english above the rio piedras
reveals abundant adventures
there is a constant of huhudiosity
from la oficina to la oficina
in search of indolent boredom
until flash floods flush sewage garbage
to dump on crowded office floors
and scampers the gurus of knowledge

teaching above the rio piedras
you will understand coleridge
as the mariner of walter raleigh
cries beneath the mossy walls:
"humidity on all walls
and all the books do stink
humidity on every wall
and everyone falls sick"

then mi compañeros y compañeras
blow fuse and break into tonguas
munching tostones of anger
bravehearts tromping defeated shadows
lurking in orange dungeons

in the corridors of defeat
our neophytes linger in hope

because they believe
in this emptiness of fullness
stranded on this Rio Piedras
where watery visions flow nowhere
and all the people say:
nosotros sommos nosotros sommos

when I query them to explain
they all chant: we are English students
if you do not get it, then nosotros sommos!!

Crushing Mangoes

driving over fallen mangoes
as they roll away in fear
hearing them pop
seeing them ooze
yellow green and pulp
makes me omnipotent

but most of all
the sweetness that darken the road
saddens me the most
saddens me for missed opportunities

because why you may ask?
Because,
the nipples not nibbled
the slurp over hidden navels
the juices down the elbow not licked
the ripe skin not pealed and licks
and oh! Oh! Mama Mia!
The smooth seed not gleaned
by tooth, tongue and lip
and after to dream beneath
the shadow of a mango tree
with a tooth pick between my teeth
and pick hairy teeth with sweet stained fingers

but I still prefer to drive over fallen mangoes
for driving over falling mangoes
makes me feel powerfully miserable

My Last Testament

I live

therefore,

when I die and sneak away
from this passion of pain
this I will to the corpse gleaners

I want to be entombed
in a womb facing monsoons
where I can ride reckless
on the wet winds of hurricanes

I want to be draped
in a spider-shaped shroud
my spirit will spiral and spin
webs and yarns to entangle
the living in their dreams of death

I must be hidden
in a crab-caged casket
so I can scurry and scratch
whoever is in my way in heaven's sand

you must cremate this supine frame
in a uterus-shaped calabash
that covers the pot of bones
left sitting at the cross-roads
where ignoramuses collide
carrying their wares to markets
bringing their buys from markets
at dusk, at dawn, at anytime

oh, you must not forget
swaddle me in umbilical cords
then intern me beneath the tamarindo

or better beneath the ceiba shade
lying across head paths
to trip the swollen feet of the defeated

sauntering to headwaters of cross-rivers
aha! I remember most of all
ye that will leap about and weep
at my sneaky departure
laugh, the bitterness of my tongue is done
laugh, the appetite of my lips is gone
laugh, the emptiness of my vision is full
laugh, the sourness of my mood is full
but give due honor to my will.